Coming Up Higher

Alfred Wright

ISBN 979-8-89243-246-7 (paperback)
ISBN 979-8-89243-247-4 (digital)

Christian Faith Publishing
832 Park Avenue
Meadville, PA 16335
www.christianfaithpublishing.com

Printed in the United States of America

CONTENTS

Introduction

I thank God for the opportunity to release some of the things that He has poured into my heart to reach out and pour into the hearts of those who have ears to hear what the Spirit is saying to the church. I have written this book to encourage the people of God to be alert and recognize all the ways the Holy Spirit is speaking to us and how important it is for us to respond to Him with our whole heart in obedience to Him, for His way is perfect and must be followed for us to continually walk in victory in this season and hour of time.

This book is born out of an answer to the call from the Lord on my wife, Rebecca, and me to come up higher. There is no question that we were joined together for the purpose of accomplishing a purpose in the heart of God that He has been preparing us for over that last twenty years even before He brought us together as husband and wife. We began to see the call of coming up higher everywhere in the Scripture, from Genesis to Revelation. The more we studied the Word, the more we saw it as a main theme from the heart of God to the people of God.

I am referring to the people of God because this call does not begin to mean anything until you give yourself to the One calling you. Many voices out there in this hour are calling us from every direction, but there is only One voice that matters. The voice that speaks to our eternal destiny versus the voices that are distracting us from that eternal destiny with the temporary things of this world that will soon pass away.

In Matthew 6:33, Jesus said, "But seek first the kingdom of God and His righteousness, and all these things shall be added to you." I pray that reading this book will cause you to begin hearing that call to your heart and help you decide that it's your turn to say, "I'm coming up higher." It will become your life's journey as you see it unfold one day at a time while you work with the Holy Spirit, Who will order your steps toward your most high place in Him.

He is faithful to do it and will not fail at what needs to be done to make it so. He wants it done more than we want it done, so we won't need to convince Him to help make it come to pass. I am excited about what the Holy Spirit is about to reveal to you as you begin to explore what it means to answer the call of "coming up higher." Amen. So be it.

Chapter 1

Taking Our Christianity to a New Level

Being a "born-again Christian" comes with great purpose and responsibility, yet many times, this very important truth is missed and delayed from being taught for many years by those teaching Christian growth. The term *born again* implies a new beginning, so one of the first things to realize is that I am going to have to learn things I have never known or understood before (Jeremiah 33:3 AMPC).

One of the first things to realize is that you now have a personal relationship with the Almighty God, the Creator, the One Who knows everything about us before we ever existed (Psalm 139:16). Even if we don't have a clue what that means, it's yet a deep-seated truth that is most important to grasp by faith early on with the same faith we used to become a born-again Christian.

The mother and father of a newborn baby want them to know who they are and whose they are, as well as that they are connected to and are part of that family unit. From that day on, the baby learns to identify with who they are and whose they are. This is what goes on in an ideal family setting, and that's why the devil works so hard to destroy that family setting, for Satan comes to steal, kill, and destroy God's ordained plan for each of us (John 10:10).

As born-again Christians, we are birthed into the family of God, and the Holy Spirit is there to teach and nurture us as baby Christians to identify with our heavenly Father and the Lord Jesus Christ, our Elder Brother, Who is our Lord, our Savior, and our King. It has now become personal as I see the Father, the Son, the Holy Spirit, and me. Yes, me. I am now a part of the whole like never before.

As revealed to us in Romans 11:17, we were like a wild olive branch grafted into the main part of the olive tree to receive the richness of its root and sap. This can be related to us as being given eternal life by being connected to the Tree of Life and the promise of life and life more abundantly, as Jesus spoke of in John 10:10b.

We live in a world that has seen and felt great pain and chaos in many ways while being robbed of the chance to belong to and identify with who they are and whose they are. That is the work of the one spoken of in John 10:10a, who is called the thief that comes to steal, kill, and destroy. Satan is the creator and owner of that part. He works to deceive the masses by redirecting our focus on one another and then ultimately toward God as the one to blame Him for our not having received what we want. Then Satan wants us to see ourselves as victims of circumstances.

This may have some validity to it if man had not been created with "human choice." In Romans 5:12–21, we see where humanity's choice of evil began. It began with one man (Adam), and the chance for all of us to choose righteousness began with the One Man (Jesus). Jesus also revealed something to us in John 8:42–44 when He was speaking to His accusers about why they desired to kill Him. They were inspired by their father—the father of lies who works against the plans and purposes of God. This is one of the main things misconceived by many Christians concerning who's to blame why bad things happen to good people. This leads to another avenue of *taking our Christianity to a new level* by having a renewed mind.

One of the main things missing in the early stages of being a born-again Christian is learning the importance of having a renewed mind. Paul speaks of this in Romans 12:2: We, as Christians, are not to be conformed to the world's ideals and opinions but be transformed by the renewing of our minds through the Word of God, which can only be done with the help of the Holy Spirit.

He is the Master Teacher Who lives within every born-again believer, showing us how to see things from God's perspective. When we are taught things through life experiences and apply God's word to it, then the revelation of knowledge will come to us through the Holy Spirit, greatly affecting the way we perceive things around us.

Some will say, "Why does it have to be such a big deal? Why does a natural baby or child have to learn early to understand who they are and whose they are?" They need to have the right mindset and surety of knowing this because it gives them a solid foundation to grow and build their life on. The Christian's foundation is the Word of God, on which our life begins, is sustained, and perfected so that we will mature as the sons of God.

As a Christian believer, if we are to fulfill our God-ordained destiny, there is no option but to have absolute trust in the absolute truth of God's Word so that we will live victoriously in Christ Jesus in this life. Psalm 138:2 (AMPC) reveals to us that God's Word and His name is "exalted above all else" and that God Himself magnifies His own Word above His own name. Psalm 119:89 concludes that the Word of God is forever settled in heaven. This implies to me that my heavenly Father is VERY serious about His Word, and it will deal with the "temporary and eternal existence" of every human being, whether we choose heaven or hell as our destiny.

I hope you caught the term *choose*, which implies choice, as we have spoken of earlier. In Psalm 119:105, we are shown that the Word of God is a lamp to our feet and a light to our path. This helps us see how to make the right choices in the moment and where we are going while walking through the dark places in this world all around us.

David said, "Yes, though I walk through the valley of the shadow of death I will fear no evil for You (Lord) are with me" (Psalm 23:4). This is our victory. The Word of God is the final authority because it is eternal, and nothing can affect or change its position of being "exalted above all else."

Again, in basic Christianity 101, we learn that after becoming born again, we must begin to grow in the grace and knowledge of our Lord and Savior, Jesus Christ (2 Peter 3:18), so we will know who we are and Whose we are. This is most important to capture because as He has chosen us, we must now choose Him as well. Salvation is a gift from God that He established through His Son, Jesus Christ, and offered to us as a package full of all that is needed for the fulfillment of the destiny that He created for us to have (Ephesians 2:7–10).

Taking our Christianity to a new level is the ongoing life journey of our Christian walk. As we learn to live through a renewed mind, we will discover that the more we learn, the more we will realize how much we don't know. This part of Christianity 101, titled "Christian Humility," leads us to each new level of our growth (1 Peter 5:6). We are instructed to humble ourselves under the mighty hand of God so that He may exalt us in due time.

I have come to learn that for some, this is hard, and for some, it is not as hard. If you are a strong-willed person, then being humble may be more of a challenge for you because it requires you to remain teachable, and those who don't like being told what to do may not surrender as easily as one who is more of a compliant-type person. There is this thing called *pride* that all of us must deal with in one way or another.

While I was writing this book, the Holy Spirit revealed something to me about Jesus. He showed me that Jesus was both strong-willed and compliant in a perfectly balanced way. Jesus was very compliant when it came to obeying and doing the Father's will, and at the same time, He was very strong-willed in His faith concerning the Father's will to the point that anyone who tried to interfere with His compliance will be sternly dealt with.

There is an example in Matthew 16:16–17 where Peter was saying something that came from the Father through him, and Jesus was in total compliance with that truth to the point of confirming it to be so. Then later in that same chapter, in verses 21 to 22, Peter began to speak again, and this time, Jesus strongly rebuked him, saying, "Get behind me, Satan." Compliant to agree with the Father and strong-willed to resist any form of doubt about the will of God for Him. We will get into more of this in the next chapter.

We all come into the family of God as babies in Christ, so as we grow up, we become a child of God, but it doesn't stop there because, as we mature in Him, we find ourselves wanting to be about the Father's business as Jesus did in Luke chapter 2.

As we continue on that path, we become sons of God through the leading of the Holy Spirit, crying Abba, Father (Romans 8:14–15). As sons, we choose the Father's business over our own desires tied to the things of the world (Satan's world system), which means that, even though we are in this world, we are not of this world operating as the world does. The renewed mindset takes us to a higher level of seeing and doing things because compliance with the Word of God orders our steps, and our faith in the Eternal Word takes us to a new level of thinking and being to get things done.

We are called to be ambassadors of Christ (2 Corinthians 5:20); therefore, because we are in this world, but not of this world, we do all things heartily as unto the Lord and not to men, knowing that from the Lord, we will receive the reward of the inheritance; for we serve the Lord Christ (Colossians 3:23–24 NKJV).

Let me explain this further. Jesus is the One Who gave us the footprint to follow as He came down from heaven's throne and lowered Himself to be in this world as a human being to show us how it is supposed to be done (Philippians 2:5–11). His focus was on the will of the Father for His life. He had a purpose to fulfill; it was the most important thing in His life because He loved the Father and us.

Therefore, He came to give His life and defeat death so that we might have the opportunity to choose life over death and become sons of God, living now in this life and eternally with Him as it was meant to be from the very beginning. In Hebrews 5:7–9, we learn that Jesus offered passionate prayers in confidence. He learned obedience through having suffered many things and walked in obedience to the Father's will despite facing Satan's many attacks against His life. He showed us that, in this life, yes, we would have trials, tribulations, distresses, and frustrations. However, because of what He did and gave us, we can have peace, confidence, and good cheer in the midst of it (John 16:33 AMPC).

As Christian believers, we identify with being in this world, but we live it as *of the kingdom* of God. So as stated earlier, "We are in this world but not of it." That is one of the reasons 2 Peter 3:18 says in his closing verse, "But grow in grace and the knowledge of our Lord and Savior Jesus Christ. To Him be glory, both now and forever."

He was sharing with us the summation of his heartfelt life experiences through having been with Jesus. Grow (increase) in grace (the empowering presence of God that enables us to *be* all that He says we are) and in the knowledge (to experience the intimacy of knowing Him) of our Lord and Savior Jesus Christ. This will create the desire to give Him glory and honor both now and forever.

As our Christianity comes to new levels, we will become more and more aware of the truth that we should glorify Him "now" in this life daily and that we will be "forever" glorifying Him in eternity. He is the Alpha and the Omega, the First and the Last, the Author and the Finisher of our faith, our Lord and King, the Holy Lamb of God, and He is the Mighty Lion of Judah, the Great I AM. All the honor and all the praise be unto the precious name of Jesus Christ, our Lord and Savior.

Amen. So be it.

Chapter 2

Getting Past Myself (My Soul)

The more I became determined to allow the Holy Spirit to show me what it really means to "come up higher," the more I realized how much of a problem "self" was to the process of that being fulfilled. The Holy Spirit began to show me how Jesus was selfless in His journey to rise into the person of being the Messiah. Jesus was not making it about Himself. He made it about His Father's will (John 5:30 AMPC). He was always revealing to them what the Father wanted them to see and know, so much so that He taught the disciples to pray as such: "Our Father Who art in heaven Hallowed be Your Name. Your kingdom come Your will be done on earth as it is in heaven" (Matthew 6:9–10).

We see Him showing us this again when He was twelve years old. Jesus and His family were in Jerusalem at a Jewish festival, and when it ended, the family began to travel back home. His parents went a day's journey out when they realized He was not with their caravan, and after going back and looking for Him for three days, they found He was at the temple with the scholars of the synagogue, asking and answering questions.

His mother asked Him, "Why did you do that to us?"

He said, "Why did you seek Me? Did you not know that I must be about My Father's business?"

At twelve years old, He was about His Father's business for three days. He was in the synagogue, separated from His parents, and not worried about not being with them on the journey home. He was not thinking about Himself even as a twelve-year-old boy. He was mindful of being about His Father's business (Luke 2:41–50).

We could look at many scriptures showing how Jesus would dictate to Himself the way He would take care of Himself and not allow other things to control that decision. In other words, before circumstances could take control of Him, He took control of them to do the Father's will through the power of the Holy Spirit.

A scripture comes to mind where He said outright that His thoughts came from the Father. John 5:19 (AMPC) shows us how He handled things. In summary, He said that He says and does nothing of Himself but only what the heavenly Father says and does.

I mentioned John 5:30 (AMPC) earlier, where He states, "I do not seek or consult My own will" (I have no desire to do what is pleasing to Myself, My own aim, My own purpose). I know that these are some strong words, and they are meant to be. Remember that the title of this book is *Coming Up Higher*, and as I am continuously reemphasizing, this is life's journey for all born-again believers.

Jesus prepared for thirty years to do three and a half years of ministry, and He was without sin the whole time. Did not consulting His own will (being done with Himself) have any bearing on Him not having sin in His life? I'll let you, as I have, think about the answer to that question even though the answer does start with a *Y* (yes).

In Matthew 16:24, Jesus said, "If anyone desires to come after Me, let him deny himself, take up his cross, and follow Me." So it appears that the first criterion required to follow Jesus is to deny *self* or be done with *self*. To be done with myself does not mean that I don't take care of myself in all the ways that I need to do; it's about who decides when, where, how, or what those ways are.

Who is in control of how you take care of yourself? Is it you or someone else, or do you just flow with whatever will be in the moment? Years ago, the Holy Spirit asked me a question that caused me to begin this journey. He said to me, "Are you leading your thoughts, or are your thoughts leading you?" At the time, I was thinking deeply about some things that were coming up, and a lot of things came to mind. So I had to begin to pay more attention to what I was allowing myself to think about as I dealt with the issues of the day and ask the Holy Spirit to help me in doing so.

Take note that when the Holy Spirit speaks to us, we need to take hold of that and treat it like a golden nugget. Treasure it as the most precious thing in your life and keep it in your heart until it accomplishes what it has been sent to do. Remember that when the Holy Spirit speaks a word to us, it is a personal word of God tailor-made for us, and it comes with purpose and the power to change everything for our good.

I decided I needed to partner with Him to help me develop a pattern of leading my thoughts versus my thoughts leading me. He has given me that ability and empowered me to be alert to what enters my mind and filter it out before it has a chance to create anything in my thoughts. As I practiced following His lead, He showed me how to see the thought coming and discern what it was going to do. Have you ever done something and afterward say, "I don't know what I was thinking when I did that"? Most of us can relate to that weird feeling that comes in that moment or after that moment. It's usually something you wish you could undo or at least do in a different way.

In Ephesians 2:10, Paul told the body of Christ at Ephesus that God has a predestined, planned purpose for our lives and that we are to fulfill it by walking it out in Christ. So Jesus showed us that to accomplish the Father's will for our lives, we're going to have to rise above our flesh-soul partnership and step into our new soul-spirit partnership that is now in place as a born-again Christian.

Romans 6:11 (TPT) lets us know, "Since you are now joined to Him, you must continually view yourselves as dead and unresponsive to sin's appeal [flesh-soul] while living daily for God's pleasure [soul-spirit] in union with Jesus, the Anointed One."

In the Scripture, we learn that we are tri-part beings—spirit, soul, and body (1 Thessalonians 5:23). Therefore, when we are born again, see it as, "I am a spirit, I have a soul, and I live in a body." Our spirit is made alive by the Holy Spirit, and we are disconnected from our old, unregenerate self and connected to the Life Source—our Father in heaven. We are then adopted into the family of God (John 3:6 AMPC, Romans 8:15 AMPC and TPT). We are empowered by the Holy Spirit to do all that the Word says for us to do.

This is part of the great salvation Paul speaks of in Hebrews 2:3 which should not be neglected or disregarded. Salvation is a gift from God the Father through His beloved

Son by the power of the Holy Spirit, released to us on the earth to receive by grace through our faith (Ephesians 2:8). In no way am I saying that this process is a piece of cake. If that were so, I don't think Jesus would have gone through all that He did to utterly defeat Satan and his wicked helpers and then send the Holy Spirit to work in us to make it so.

Yes, He works in us to make it so because we would utterly fail without the Helper, Comforter, Counselor, Strengthener, Advocate, Intercessor, and Standby. Yes, the Holy Spirit is all that and so much more. Jesus made it perfectly clear that He *had* to go back to send the Holy Spirit to us (John 16:7 AMPC). Then He instructed them to go to the upper room and wait for the Holy Spirit to come, for when He comes, they shall receive power and be His witnesses (Acts 1:8).

Some Christians don't have a clue how important it is to build a relationship and have fellowship with the Holy Spirit daily. Not being aware of this leaves the enemy a lot of room to distort and hinder growth along their Christian journey. The Holy Spirit is in us to help us grow in grace and knowledge of our Lord and Savior (2 Peter 3:18). He is the Master Teacher, the very presence of God in us, Who is greater in us than he who is in the world (1 John 4:4).

I like to see Him as the *super* on my natural, making me a supernatural being on earth. I am a man of God because I am a man joined to God inside of me, and as He gives me more and more revelation of that truth, I capture those truths, and I find myself being just that—a man of God. He will not fail to make it so if I will only say, "Yes, Lord," and allow Him to work in every area of my life.

He loves working with us, from the little things to the impossible things in our life, because He is personal like that and is *well* able to handle any situation we may have. Think about it. He created the universe, so what do I have going on in my life that He cannot handle? All knowing, all-powerful, and always present—yes! Our God is an awesome God and delights in spending time with us. It's amazing how He has opened the way for us to come boldly to the throne of grace to receive mercy and help us in a time of need (Hebrews 4:16).

We are never without the answer needed to walk in victory and flourish in the resolve He provides us with. I've said to the many people to whom I've ministered that He has a million ways to resolve one of our problems perfectly, and all we have to do is allow one of His one million ways to handle it. One common factor in what I have been saying is that to fulfill coming up higher in my Christian life,

I must continue to get past myself (my soul) and declare, "Father, Your will be done."

The issue of understanding and dealing with the soul is one that every Christian will have to major in to live in freedom and walk in victory while living on this earth. I am not trying to do a word study on the word *soul*, but I must at least mention some of its meaning so it will be more relevant to some readers.

The word *soul* is *nephesh* in Hebrew and is defined as life, breath, self, person, mind, personality, inner desires, and feelings. There are times when the word *heart* is usually used when referring to the inner man, yet it is used most often to describe the whole person instead of just the inner person. The Greek word for *soul* is *Psuche* defined as the lower region of man's being, the immaterial part of man. It is also considered the seat of our affections, will, desire, emotions, mental reasoning, understanding, and inner self or essence of life.

The soul is distinguished from the spirit of man, which is what directly connects us with being made in the image of God. God is a Spirit, and we are spirit beings; we have a soul, and we live in a body (Genesis 2:7). The animals have a soul and a body, but they do not have a spirit, so human beings are of a higher order in God's creation, having been made in His image as a spirit being. We will cover more of this in the next chapter as well.

Jesus said in John 10:17, "I lay down My life [soul] that I may take it up again." He laid down His soul, which was His mind, His will, and His emotions that the Father's will may be done. He walked in total obedience to the Father's will by laying down His life and denying and being done with Himself.

I spoke of this earlier in the chapter about Jesus being selfless in His daily walk. This was His way of showing us that we would have to do the same thing through the power of the Holy Spirit. Paul comes later in Philippians 2:12 and tells us that we must work out our own (soul) salvation in fear and trembling. The AMPC expands this, saying that this means "self-distrust, with serious caution, tenderness of conscience, watchfulness against temptation, timidly shrinking from whatever might offend God and discredit the name of Christ."

This is a powerful insight to meditate on, and it begins with "self-distrust," which is denying myself, being done with myself, and getting past myself. Now look at verse 13, the next verse, and see how it starts. It begins by saying, "Not in your own strength" (AMPC); in other words, this is not to be done in self, "for it is God Who is all the while effectually at work in you." Over and over again, I see the

Scripture saying that I must get past myself for the Holy Spirit to freely be effectually at work in me. This implies that we could be in the way of the work of the Holy Spirit in our lives because we want it our way.

We want the blessing, but we want it our way; we want healing, but we want it our way; we want prosperity, but we want it our way; we want to flow in the ministry anointing and the power of God, but we want it our way. As human beings, depending on our personality, makeup, and how we were taught growing up, turning that attitude around could be a struggle because of the strong habits and inclinations we have trained ourselves to be. That's why we need to partner with the Holy Spirit and let Him take control of our transformation process. Learn to love the process, His presence, and His intervention in the affairs of our lives, however great or small. The Holy Spirit will empower us to *be* all that we are supposed to *be* and then help us accomplish it if we will allow Him to take that lead.

He is faithful to never let go of us as we learn to flow in the unforced rhythms of grace. The Father loves us unconditionally, and He just won't quit because He already knows every weakness, flaw, sin, and unforgivable thing (in our estimation) that we have done (past), are yet doing (present), or are going to do (future). God is love, and He has already sent His Son to deal with all those things so we can receive forgiveness and be free if we just ask.

Our way out is to come all the way into His perfect way of being and doing. Our lives are priceless to Him, and He has made a way of escape through His Son, Jesus. In Galatians 5:16 (AMPC), we are shown a path to follow, and if we take it to heart, we will find ourselves coming up higher sooner than later. It states, "But I say, walk and live [habitually] in the Holy Spirit [responsive to and controlled and guided by the Spirit]; then you will certainly not gratify the cravings and desires of the flesh [of human nature without God]." In short, we are to focus on being obedient to the Holy Spirit, which will empower us to be more resistant to the desires of the flesh. Most of the time, we are too busy fighting that old dead man called the flesh instead of learning to live the good life destined for us in Christ Jesus (Ephesians 2:10).

The soul is a part of us that is being saved through the process of sanctification after we receive our salvation, and our spirit man has been born again, as we mentioned earlier in the chapter, as it speaks of in John 3:6. Jesus said to Nicodemus, "What is born of the flesh is the flesh and what is born of the Spirit is the spirit." In short, He was saying that our spirit is what is born again and made alive by the power of the Holy Spirit as He reconnects us to the life source of God the Father as it was in the beginning before Adam and Eve sinned.

When Adam sinned, it created a shift in the original design, putting the soul at the top of the ruling force in man, with the flesh as its motivator to do things—whether good or evil—depending on what was in the heart at the time. Everything in life is a matter of the heart, as it is from the heart that all the issues of life originate. The heart is the center of our being and the place that God looks at when he sees us (Proverbs 4:23, 1 Samuel 16:7).

The soul gathers up all our experiences and gives our heart things to build a foundation for our belief system. This is what causes us to be most often our own worst enemy as we resist and rebel against the work of the Holy Spirit because one of His names is the Helper. He is the only One Who exactly knows what to do to help us, but He can't do that without our permission and our obedience to do so.

Remember, the soul is the seat of our mind, will, emotions, and intellectual reasoning. That's one of the reasons that Proverbs 22:6 tells us to train up a child in the way they should go because as they get older, those values will come back to them. All the things we learn early on take root in our hearts and souls and are hard to change once they have been accepted as the truth or the normal way of living our lives.

The scripture above, Proverbs 4:23, strongly emphasizes that we are to keep and guard our hearts, which is not the norm in today's culture. I am sure you have heard and maybe even said to someone, "Just follow your heart," when they were trying to decide something. That all sounds good and well until we see what has been put into that person's heart to use as the guiding wisdom.

Jeremiah 17:9–10 reveals something to us that many wouldn't find easy to agree with because they think that people's hearts are basically good. God, Who created the heart and soul, knows something that we don't, and since the fall of Adam, the heart and soul are liable to go north and south at the same time because a double-minded person is unstable in all their ways (James 1:8).

What is a double-minded person? In this verse, the context refers to a doubter or wavering person who can't make up their mind; one version uses the term *halfhearted*. This person is often uneasy, restless, and not at peace about things in their lives; they battle with the place of living in faith or living in fear of the *what-ifs* in life. First John 4:16–19 tells us that God gives us His perfect love, and when we get the revelation of that perfect love, it will cast out all fear.

God is love, and love waits for us to receive Him into every area of our lives with our whole hearts.

Several years back, the Lord spoke something to me. He said this:

> Stop trying to fix, repair, or rebuild what I have crucified. Yes, I'm speaking of your old self. I have removed the veil from your face so that you may now see the bright glory of My face looking at you. In that place, you will see and know that My great love for you is not about the old you, but it's about the new image that you now have that is being transfigured from one bright level of glory to the next. This is what I am doing with you, in you, and to you with great joy and pleasure. I delight in watching you grow in My grace and the knowledge of Who I am in every area of your life. All of this comes from the Lord, Who is the Spirit. Yes, the Spirit of the Lord is the Holy Spirit, Who is with you now and forever more. He is the Master Teacher, He is the Enabler, and He is all that everyone will ever need. So be the

first to partake of Him, for He is the only True Source of Life on earth. He waits to be welcomed like a lover who desires to be with you more and more as He pours out more and more grace [power of the Holy Spirit] to deal with anything that inter-feres with you and Him being together. He wants that more than you do.

This is one way to show how the heart of God is always reaching out to our hearts to show His great love because that's Who He is and what He does. The grace of God has been released into the earth and cannot be diminished, but faith is the only way to receive all the benefits of what grace has been sent to do.

With all of this being said, it stands to reason that mankind needs help to deal with life's heart issues, for we cannot fix everything that's wrong in ourselves, let alone what is in the hearts of others. I remember reading in Ezekiel 36:26 how God said He would give us a new heart and put a new spirit within us. He will remove the heart of stone and will give us a heart of flesh. We will discuss this more in the next chapter as we discover what God means when He draws us into life's journey of "coming up higher."

Amen. So be it unto us just as You have said.

Chapter 3

Making All Things New

In the process of "coming up higher," getting past myself really helps me see things from a totally different perspective. I can now see Him working more than ever, and I realize that what He is doing is making all things new. This is what Jesus said in Revelation 21:5: "I AM making all things new." Why not? He is the Creator.

This has been happening since He came into the earthly realm as Immanuel, which means "God became one of us." He was among humanity, and at that time, humanity was being driven by the world system. Little did they know that things were about to change and never be the same again.

Immanuel came to make all things new, for He was and is and is to come as the Alpha and the Omega, the Beginning and the End, the First and the Last, and we could go on (Revelation 1:8, 11a). Therefore, the Creator of all things came to implement the plans that would restore things to the divine order that was corrupted by Adam's decision to disobey God's one command to not eat of the tree of the knowledge of good and evil. For in the day that you eat of it, you will surely die (Genesis 2:17–18).

Jesus came to be the last Adam to restore life where death was now ruling. Through Jesus Christ, God's life was sent into the earthly realm so that we may behold God with us and see firsthand the glory of God's presence among men while He was becoming one of us (Luke 1:34–35).

A lot had happened through the posterity of the first Adam that was not in the plan of God's perfect will for mankind. He knew it would happen and prepared for things to be resolved while making all things new in the process. Jesus was born sinless because He was not of the posterity of the first Adam's seed but of the Holy Spirit, and He came to create a whole new Christ kind of man while eventually bringing the old Adam man to an end (1 Corinthians 15:48–49).

Since we are now a Christ man, we are redeemed from the curse of the first Adam man and liberated from the law of sin and death (Galatians 3:13, Romans 8:1–2). We have received the divine nature of our Father God and have been given the power and the authority to become sons of God (John 1:12). Christ, after one sacrifice, took care of our sins and consecrated a new and living way for us through His flesh that we may now come before the Father freely and confidently, knowing that we are accepted in the beloved.

The Holy Spirit is our witness to all of this as He speaks of the new covenant where He is putting the laws of God in our hearts and the Word in our minds, and our sins are forgiven and forgotten forever (Hebrews 10:14–20). Jesus created a new and eternal blood covenant for us to have access to because that covenant is between Him and the Father, and because we are in Christ, we have all the benefits of that covenant as well. We have also become heirs of all that He has in the Father. All His promises to us are yes and amen (2 Corinthians 1:20). By faith, we have been given all that the kingdom of God has to offer us, and ultimately, we get to rule and reign with Him throughout all eternity.

This is all part of the package of salvation that was given to us as a gift from God. It is what Jesus and the Father, being the great Mediator between God and man, came to do for us (1 Timothy 2:5–6). The truth of the matter is that it really does reveal to us that He is "Making All Things New," and we, as born-again Christians, are products of that ongoing process.

How often, as born-again Christians, do we take note of the truth that we have been made new? Being born again begins when our spirit man is made alive, and the new life of God fills our being for the first time.

Romans 6:10–11 gives us a snapshot of what we are to focus on now that we are born again. In those verses, we see that Paul is instructing us to focus on our new life in the spirit man and practice being dead to the old man, knowing that its power over us is broken. We are now a new man in Christ Jesus with the Spirit of grace living in us, empowering us to *be* all that He says we are as a new man in Christ Jesus. We need to be excited about that and be full of confidence that He Who has begun a good work in us will continue until the day that Jesus Christ returns. He will develop us, sanctify us, and complete and perfect us for His glory (Hebrews 13:20–21). He wants this more than we do, and the Father is pleased to make it so to honor His Son's sacrifice and bring glory to His name. He wants us to experience unbroken fellowship with the Holy Spirit, and the Holy Spirit yearns with a jealous love to be welcomed into every area of our lives.

This is an intense thing with Him, so much so that He continues to give us more and more grace (more of His power) to choose Him, humble ourselves to do His will, and receive His great love (James 4:5–6 AMPC). Each day we live is a new day, and it is provided by the very One Who put us here in the first place. So with that being said, what do you think would honor Him as a response to His great love for giving us another new day? How about Psalm 118:24 for starters: "This is the day the Lord has made. We will rejoice and be glad in it." I like to emphasize the word *will* because it shows that I have chosen to rejoice in what my Father has done. He made a new day for me to live in and have a brand-new start at living life again one day at a time.

We are trying so hard to deal with the past and prepare for the future that we often don't realize the present moment before us. We live in a world/culture crowded every moment of the day with something being said, someplace to go, or something to see or to do. Why do we need twenty-four hours of news? Is it really news, and is it even newsworthy? Access to all that is around the world 24-7, 365 days a year, and then we begin a new year and start all over again.

Have you ever said, Where did the time go? Where did the day go? Where did the week go? Where did the month go? Where did the year go? Here we go again! Life is daily, not yearly, because honestly, in the reality of things, we can only take one day at a time. No matter how we look at it, the past is gone, the future is coming, and here we are right now in the present moment, planning how to live in the next moment.

There is a story in Luke 12:16–23. Jesus told about a certain rich man who had so much produce that he could not contain it, so he said, "I will build more barns and store more and more of my goods. I will say to my soul, 'Sit back and eat, drink, and be merry for years to come.'" Then God said to Him, "Foolish man, this night, death shall require your soul and then to whom will your goods belong." He had planned for the future and was loathing over his past successes and didn't realize that the present moment upon him was there for the last time.

This is a sobering story because most of us know someone who has followed that path and had a sudden ending. The real question is, Are we on that path where we are consumed with this life and unaware of what our destiny is in Him and even more so with Him? He has come to make all things new for us one day at a time so we can have a fresh start if we choose to do so. He has given us His great grace, great love, great mercy, and great peace, and He gave us the Holy Spirit to bring us into all that He has for us so that all our need would be met according to His riches in glory (2 Peter 1:3–4, Philippians 4:19). This is part of His process, making all things new. He is always working to show us that this is what He has come to do for anyone who will allow Him to do so in their lives. He has it all worked out, but it requires us to say, "Yes, Lord," to His way of doing it.

In Colossians 3:1–4 (AMPC), Paul shows us that because we are risen with Christ (to a new life), we are to seek the things above where Christ is seated—at the right hand of God. These verses begin by giving us a new life with Christ and then letting us know how we are to focus on the new perspective we've been given from above, where

Christ is seated—at the right hand of God. In verse 2, we are exhorted to set our minds and keep them set on the things above (the higher things) and not on the things on earth. We are dead to the old and alive to the new life hidden with Christ in God because now, when Christ, Who is our life, appears, we will also appear with Him in His glory (vv. 3–4).

Being made new is what we have inherited from and through the finished works of Jesus Christ. This is shown to us by Paul in 2 Corinthians 5:17–21 (AMPC), declaring that if any man is in Christ, he is a new creature/creation, and the old things have passed away; behold, all things have become new.

Here we are again. He is making all things new in each person who comes into Him. This sounds like if you really want to experience newness in life, then you can find it in Christ. Verse 18 lets us know that all things are from God, Who, through Jesus Christ, has reconciled us to Himself, and now He has given us the ministry of reconciliation so that we may help bring others into this newness of life as well.

Christ reconciled us to Himself so He could cancel our sins and trespasses, restoring us to have favor with our God and Father. In verse 21, it reveals that God made Christ to be our sin who knew no sin, and He took it away so that we could now qualify to be made the righteousness of God in Christ Jesus. He got rid of the old me to create the new me in Christ, where nothing could ever separate me from His love again (Romans 8:31–39). What Adam did in the beginning to create that separation has been restored and reconciled by our Lord Jesus Christ once and for all (Romans 5:17–19).

I mentioned in the last chapter that when we are born again, the spirit of man is directly affected. Jesus spoke of this when He talked to Nicodemus in John 3:3 and 6, explaining to us how that works. Since our spirit is the candle of the Lord, searching all the inward parts of our heart (Proverbs 20:27), we need to see our spirit man, now alive through the new birth, beginning to work that way on our behalf.

Why do you think, as a new Christian, you are now beginning to know that something is different in awareness of all around you? You may not have total clarity about what's going on at that time, but the reality of your new birth will become more and more real to you as you get into the Word of God.

The spirit man continues searching and examining to manifest itself through our increased revelation—knowledge of God's Word. In Hebrews 4:12 (AMPC), we learn that the living Word of God is sharper than any two-edged sword, and it is alive and full of power to the dividing line of the spirit, soul, and body. It also says that it affects the deepest parts of our nature, exposing, sifting, analyzing, and judging our heart's very thoughts and purposes.

Looking at the way these scriptures flow together, it is not hard to realize how important it is to bathe our newborn spirit man in the living water of God's Word and trust the Holy Spirit to make us what we ought to be as He searches us through and through. This is a process that becomes our daily journey as Christians. As I have said before, life happens one day at a time, and we must learn to live it one day at a time. Jesus said in Matthew 6:34 (TPT), "Refuse to worry about tomorrow, but deal with each challenge that comes your way, one day at a time. Tomorrow will take care of itself."

Each day has troubles of its own that is enough for that day, so we must allow the Holy Spirit to empower us to walk in victory each day. He is with us in a fresh and new way every single day with His great grace, great love, full of mercy, and the overflowing peace of God, enabling us to continue to be victorious through the finished works of Christ. We can start by saying, "This is a fresh and new day that He has made, and I will choose to rejoice and be glad in it" (Psalm 118:24, paraphrased). Our God is about making all things new, and He will do it for us all if we put

His word first, believe it, and make it the final authority. It is a matter of our choice to receive it by faith and give thanks for His faithfulness in doing it. He watches over His Word to perform it (Jeremiah 1:12).

Jesus gave us all that is needed to accomplish our purpose and destiny in this life, and we must make it our priority to partner with Him to see its manifestation in our lives. In Psalm 138:2 (AMPC), we see that God has exalted His name and His word above all else, and He has magnified His word above all His name. If God has magnified His word above all His name, then how much more should we exalt His word over all of our life, spirit, soul, and body?

The Word is what created all things new in the beginning, and it will be what makes all things new in us, for us, and through us to the glory of God. If you need all things to be made new in your life, then I invite you to come to the One Who is seated on the throne and said, "I make all things new." He is talking to whosoever will hear Him and come in faith to receive what He has made available for them.

Praise be to God, Who has promised it, Who has been faithful to do it, and then Who sealed it by giving us the gift of the Holy Spirit as well. Glory be to our Lord Jesus Christ and God our Father, Who art in heaven. He is good!

Amen. So be it.

Chapter 4

Being a *Christian*

I am very excited about expressing myself as a Christ*ian* versus a Christian. I am not trying to take anything away from being called a Christian because I know the true biblical definition of a Christian has never changed. Yet because of all the ways religion and the worldview have tried to redefine and restructure the meaning of a Christian to fit man's ideology, I must take a stand and at least address some of the basic truths of our Christianity because of the cultural shifts we see that are trying to take place.

The basic definition of a Christian is one who is a follower of Christ, so let's see how He defines *follower*. I touched on Matthew 16:24 (TPT) in chapter 2, where Jesus said to His disciples, "If you truly want to follow me, you should at once completely reject and disown your own life. And you must be willing to share my cross and experience it as your own as you continually surrender to my ways."

Wow, just reading this verse makes me examine myself to see how much I really am a Christian. Then I remembered a few things Jesus also said that helped me understand how this must be done.

In John 5:19 (APMC), Jesus said about Himself, "I assure you, most solemnly I tell you, the Son is able to do nothing of Himself [of His own accord]; but He is able to only do what He sees the Father doing, for whatever the Father does is what the Son does in the same way [in His turn]." In this verse, Jesus reveals that "the Son is able to nothing of Himself." If Jesus Himself speaks of not doing anything of Himself, then as a follower/disciple of Christ, I would have to declare the same thing for myself. I can do nothing of myself, so I look to the leading of the Holy Spirit, Who has been sent to teach me and guide me through this life's journey of being a Christian.

He spoke of this concerning us in John 16:13 (AMPC), where He said that the Holy Spirit would tell us whatever He hears from the Father, and He will announce and declare to us the things to come (will happen in our future). If Jesus, as the Son of Man, had to depend on the Holy Spirit to empower Him to fulfill His purpose and destiny as the coming Messiah, how much more do we need the enabling power of the Holy Spirit (grace) to fulfill our purpose and destiny that He has given us to be followers of Christ (Ephesians 2:10)?

The Lord is going to fulfill His will in our lives without question if we will commit ourselves to being a Christ*ian*. In Hebrews 12:1–2 (NKJV), we are given an insight into this truth. We begin by working with the Holy Spirit (v. 1) to lay aside every weight and sin that so easily ensnares us and let us run with endurance the race set before us. This race we are to run is akin to the purpose and destiny given to us by the Father, and we partner with the Holy Spirit to *be* all that *He* intends for us to *be*. This must be the heart's desire of those who declared themselves to be followers of Christ—Christ*ian*.

Once we make up our minds to be Christians, He will begin the process of making us be what He has already planned for us to be. Our heavenly Father sees us as having already accomplished this, so He has no problem being our enabler to bring His plans in us to completion (Jeremiah 29:11–13).

Hebrews 12:2 seals this truth by pointing us to Jesus, Who is the author and finisher of our faith. He is the source of our faith, and He brings it to full maturity, completion, and perfection. He will finish what He has begun in us, as He has already planned to do. He has not changed His mind about who He created us to be (Psalm 139:16), and now that Jesus has become the Atoning Sacrifice and accomplished our redemption through the blood covenant, we have been given the authority to become sons/children of God through our faith in Him (John 1:12).

Being a Christ*ian* has never been more possible than when Jesus, in the last part of Hebrews 12:2, says, "For the joy that was set before Him[Me], He[I] endured the cross, despising the shame, and He[I] is[am] now seated at the right hand of the throne of God." In this position, we are given access to the Father just like Jesus because we have been made to be joint heirs (sharing His inheritance) with Him, and this has been sealed for us by the witness of the Holy Spirit as spoken of in Romans 8:14–17.

God is good, and He wants His sons and daughters to desire to be with Him in every way as He desires to be with us in every way. Our heavenly Father loves us and wants His love to overflow in our hearts so much so that the enemy can't find a place to enter without running into the barrier of God's perfect love. His Love never fails, and this love is the reason God sent His only begotten Son to a hopeless, dying world, saving us from ourselves (1 Corinthians 13:8, John 3:16, Matthew 16:24).

Why doesn't the world accept the gift of love from God? In 2 Corinthians 4:4, Paul tells us that the god of this world (Satan) has blinded the minds of the unbeliever—

yes, their minds—so they won't see or comprehend the light of the gospel of Jesus Christ and believe. This means that they have been blinded in their understanding and kept from comprehending the truth of the gospel they have seen and heard.

If you were in a very dark place and in desperate need of some light to see where you were going, would you accept a flashlight, lantern, candlelight, or any source of light that would give you the ability to see and comprehend where you were and where you were going? That would be the normal resolve. But what if you were in the dark but didn't know that the flashlight, lantern, candlelight, and other light sources were right before you? These would help you resolve the problem of being in darkness, but you could not comprehend what you were being told about the light sources right there before you.

God has sent the Holy Spirit to draw us into the light (Jesus) so that we can see and comprehend the gift of love that has been sent to free us from the curse of sin and death (Romans 8:2). The Holy Spirit is God presently in the earth, and He is here to call out, empower, and establish the Christ*ian* to *be* a light amid darkness in the earth for Christ's sake. This can only be done if we are willing to say, "Yes, Lord," when He calls us to be His light on earth, for we are the representatives of only One Source, Jesus Christ, Who is the light of the world.

The Holy Spirit's job is also to reveal all the truth the Father has sent us. In John 14:6, Jesus said, "I am the Way, the Truth, the Life. No one comes to the Father except through Me." When *the* is used, it implies a definite article to the noun following. The way, the truth, the life definitely pertains to *the* Christ, and there is no other way, truth, or life that can lead you to God the Father. Those other options can only lead you away from the Father.

Being a Christ*ian is* simply one way of focusing the emphasis on the One Who is our Leader, our Lord and Savior. In John 12:32 (AMPC), Jesus said, "And I, if and when I be lifted up from the earth [on the cross], will draw and attract all men [Gentiles as well as Jews] to Myself." Jesus is giving us the perception of how the world would see Him from that time forward; they would see and remember Him on the cross. He would be the focal point of hope and redemption for the entire world to see and have access to. That's why the Holy Spirit comes to fill each Christ*ian* and empowers us to be witnesses of the risen Lord and lift Him for all to see and know that Jesus is Lord.

I am grateful for the work of the Holy Spirit in me because, as a Christ*ian,* I can do nothing without Him, but with Him, "I have strength for all things in Christ Who empowers me [I am ready for anything and equal to any-thing through Him Who infuses inner strength into me; I am self-sufficient in Christ's sufficiency]" (Philippians 4:19 AMPC).

As my wife, Rebecca, loves to say, "The Holy Spirit is WELL able to do what the Word says in our lives." All He needs is for us to trust Him to BE GOD on earth and in us as He was sent to BE. He has a million ways to fix each of our life situations, but He requires us to come in alignment with His way of doing it. All of the one million ways will perfectly work in handling each of our situations, yet He's looking for us to agree with Him, allowing just one of them to be activated in our situation. He is patient with us because He sees and knows all things about us and why we don't always jump on board to let Him have His way.

He is gentle and kind, yet He is the Almighty God and the One Who empowered Jesus to accomplish all that He did as the Son of Man. When we say WWJD (what would Jesus do?), it can also be seen as WDTHSDTJ (what did the Holy Spirit do through Jesus?). He was right there all the time, working the works of the Father in Jesus, His Son.

Jesus was on point in all He did because He didn't deviate from the working of the Holy Spirit in Him, Who orchestrated the Father's will in and through Him. We spoke of that in John 5:19 (AMPC), but look at verse 30 where Jesus makes an even more compelling statement about His complete surrender to the Father's will being done. He says,

> I am able to do nothing from Myself [independently, of My own accord—but only as I am taught by God and as I get His orders]. Even as I hear, I judge [I decide as I am bidden to decide. As the voice comes to Me, so I give a decision], and My judgement is right [just, righteous], because I do not seek or consult My own will [I have no desire to do what is pleasing to Myself, My own aim, My own purpose] but only the will and pleasure of the Father Who sent Me.

I know there are a lot of details in this one scripture, and it takes a bit of concentration to follow all that's being said here. However, if you take the time to do that, you'll realize it was well worth it to see the heart of Christ revealed in great detail like this. It's the revealed scriptures like this that make me realize how much I need the Holy Spirit to help me in "coming up higher."

As a Christian living in today's culture, I am convinced that if I don't get in position and buckle down in all the loose or uncertain areas of my life, then I am setting myself up for a rude awakening as a gross and dense darkness comes upon the earth (Isaiah 60:1–3 AMPC). As you read those three verses, you will see that the answer to the problem is spelled out to the born-again Christ*ian*. We are being called to arise from-to—yes, from-to, just like Jesus—from death to life, from descending into the Sheol (hell) to ascending to the highest place beside the Father in heaven. We are called to arise from the darkness to the light because the light is our original destiny.

Being a Christ*ian* or a true, biblically defined follower of Christ in today's culture requires me to be prepared for what's coming. We were born in this dispensation of time by the will of God and placed on earth wherever we are with the same call as the next person—that is, to fulfill the destiny that the Lord has prepared for us and walk it out.

This was spoken of a little in chapter 2 and earlier in this chapter, where Ephesians 2:10 states that God has a plan in place, putting us in His perfect will while on earth to flow in the blessing as He had originally intended. We are called to be partakers of the divine nature of our God and Creator to participate in the excellence of His great love and His goodness for all of mankind. To bring us to that place, He had to deal with what I call the sin factor.

If we look back at Ephesians 2:8–10, it covers the basis of that plan and how He provided total access to our salvation as His love gift to us. It begins with our salvation and settles us into His preplanned destiny for our lives, as I spoke of earlier.

I can't begin to imagine what it would mean to be in this world without Christ as my life source. As I have told others before, without Christ, I would be experiencing the true meaning of *The Walking Dead*. Life originated from God and, therefore, is maintained by the same. Apostle Paul made a statement in Acts 17:28: "For in Him we live, and move, and have our being." On a dark note, that is one of the reasons that going to hell is called eternal death because that person will be eternally separated from God and, therefore, from the Source of Life. Forever existing in a state of death or forever living in the presence of life— yes, hell or heaven is the choice we will all make one way or another, and no one can make it for you. No one! Hebrews 9:27–28 (TPT) says,

> Every human being is appointed to
> die once, and then to face God's judge-
> ment. But when we die we will be face-

to-face with Christ, the One Who experienced death once for all to bear the sins of many! And now to those who eagerly await Him, He will appear a second time; not to deal with sin, but to bring us the fullness of salvation.

The verdict will be declared at that time, depending on the choice you and I made before death's appointment. God is a loving God, but He is also a just God, and justice will be served based on the choices everyone makes before they die. Someone may say, "I don't believe that." Well, let me put it this way for you: If what I am saying turns out to be not true, then all I will miss out on is not living my life doing things the world's way, and in the end, there will be nothing of consequence either way. I'm off into oblivion. But if what I am saying is the truth, then we will have to go back to Hebrews 9:27 and say it all over again. Know this: "God is not a man that He should lie" (Numbers 23:19), and His word will not return to Him void but will accomplish that for which He sends it (Isaiah 55:11).

So I encourage you to pause and think about your appointment as spoken of in Hebrews 9:27, which is coming up in your life one day, and see if you have taken the right path and are making the right choices. Make sure you have received your gift of salvation. Yes, the one with your name on it. Join me in "coming up higher." Make it your determined purpose to take the bold stance of being a Christ*ian* in this world of constant cultural change so that, when you do face the Lord at judgment, it will be as in Matthew 25:23: "His Lord said to him, 'Well done, good and faithful servant; You have been faithful over a few things, I will make you ruler over many things. Enter into the joy of your Lord.'"

Remember that it is not about us but what our Lord Jesus has done to present the package of salvation and the Spirit of truth—yes, the Holy Spirit Himself, Who comes into us when we accept Jesus as Lord and Savior. He will perform the work in us to be a Christ*ian* on that day. Thanks be to God, Who is faithful to do it, for He is the God Almighty, Whose power no foe can withstand. Amen. So be it.

Chapter 5

The Kingdom Mindset

Fulfilling my desire to be a Christ*ian*, as I covered in chapter 4, cannot take place without being determined to commit to pursuing it wholeheartedly. It is not something that can be accomplished out of a halfhearted attempt. If I were trying out for the football team or any sports team, they would be looking for someone who is putting their whole heart into the practice and has the desire to be part of a winning team. They would be considered to be given a position on the first string. Why would we think it would take any less than giving our whole heart to pursue the will of God for our lives? King David said something that shows how his heart was all for his God. We find it in Psalm 119:9–11 (AMPC):

How shall a young man cleanse his way? By taking heed and keeping watch [on himself] according to Your word [con-forming his life to it].

With my whole heart have I sought You, inquiring for and of You and yearn-ing for You; Oh, let me not wander or step aside [either in ignorance to willfully] from Your commandments.

Your word have I laid up in my heart, that I might not sin against You.

These scriptures have really stirred my heart, urging me toward partnering with the work of the Holy Spirit in me. I want to be all that the Lord died for, giving His life and rising from the dead in victory, allowing me to fulfill what the Father had ordained for me to be before I was ever born (Jeremiah 29:11, Psalm 139:16).

Therefore, as we continue to look into the Word of God, we will see a continuous theme of how we must med-itate on His Word so that it will be in us and we will abide in it (John 15:4, 7). If we study the life of Christ, we will see that He kept preaching that the kingdom of heaven / kingdom of God is at hand, and He taught many parables describing what it is like. Christ has the kingdom mindset, and He came to reveal it to us in a way that we could be partakers of the kingdom.

One example of those parables about the kingdom is in Mark 4:30–32, where He speaks of the kingdom of God being like the mustard seed. It is the tiniest seed of all, but when it grows up to full size, it becomes the largest plant in the garden, with so many large branches spreading outward that even the birds will build nests in its shade. Jesus has sown the seed of the kingdom, and now it is springing up and growing all over the world, and no one will be able to stop it from growing.

Throughout the history of mankind, many have tried to stop the plan of God along with the help of the evil one who has been trying even before the beginning of mankind. However, God, Who has all authority and all power and is on the throne on high, knows what the evil one's plan is before it ever begins and has already made it to no effect of changing His Word. The plan of God is already completed from start to finish and just playing out what must BE.

We know it is written, "As surely as I Am the Living God, I tell you: Every knee will bow before me, and every tongue will confess the truth and glorify Me!" (Romans 14:11 TPT). This statement is the eternal word of God that cannot be changed any more than we can escape that appointment with death. At some point, everybody will face death, and no one can escape that appointment, for "it is written."

Whether I believe it or not is not final for the Word because it stands by itself, but it is final for me because I was created by that same Word. The created ones do not dictate to the Creator what will or will not be. Psalm 37:12–13 reveals to us that the Lord laughs at those who walk in the path of wickedness because He knows their end. It may seem like evil is winning sometimes, but God has the last word, and they will reap what they have sown; it is a Law of the kingdom, the Word of God. We see this law given in Galatians 6:7–8 (AMPC),

> Do not be deceived and deluded and misled; God will not allow Himself to be sneered at [scorned, disdained, or mocked by mere pretensions or professions, or by His precepts being set aside]. [He inevitably deludes himself who attempts to delude God.] For whatever a man sows, that and that only is what he will reap.
>
> For he who sows to his own flesh [lower nature, sensuality] will from the flesh reap decay and ruin and destruction, but he who sows to the Spirit will from the Spirit reap eternal life.

This scripture starts with a strong negative connotation but ends with a very positive resolve for the one who sows to the Spirit or is doing the works of righteousness.

If you look back at everything I have written so far in this chapter, you will begin to see why, as born-again Christians, we must develop the kingdom mindset to flow with and in the divine plan of God for our lives in this hour we are living in. Jesus said that the kingdom of God is within us (Luke 17:21). This means that we take the kingdom of God with us everywhere we go.

This should not be strange because Jesus also said in John 14:16–17 that the Holy Spirit, Whom the Father will send, would be in us and abide there forever. Therefore, being a Christian, everywhere we go and in everything we do, the kingdom of God is there. The Holy Spirit is present as well, no matter what we are doing—whether it is good or bad. They are both there.

This understanding should instill enough fear of God in us to honor and respect Him in what we do, where we go, what we say, and yes, even what we think about in our hearts. This is a "Selah" moment. (Pause in His presence and think about it.) As an example, Jesus said in Matthew 5:28, "Whosoever looks at a woman to lust for her has already committed adultery with her in his heart." So with that being said, it is most important to develop a kingdom mindset to understand how things work in the kingdom versus how they work in the world.

In 1 Corinthians 2:15–16, the apostle Paul shows us that the spiritual-minded person tries and examines all things, yet they are not put on trial or judged by anyone but God. Who knows the mind of the Lord or how to instruct Him? But we have the mind of Christ—His thoughts, feelings, and purposes of His heart. (Some of these wordings come from the AMPC version.) Paul is telling us to think about things from Christ's perspective, for He was always looking beyond the surface value of things and seeing what the Father saw. We must let the Holy Spirit do His part being in us as Jesus said He would in John 14:26 (NKJV): "But the Helper, the Holy Spirit, whom the Father will send in My name, He will teach you all things, and bring to your remembrance all things that I said to you."

The Holy Spirit is the Master Teacher, and we are His students. He is our Personal Counselor and Tutor, Who knows all things, sees all things, and is always present. Before we were born, He knew every situation we'd ever face and had a plan to handle it already, working it out to perfection. Let us press into being led by Him and make it our new everyday normal while rejoicing in His magnificence and excellent way of handling our day-to-day life.

One day at a time, grow in this desire and expectation of His awesome presence, giving you insight and wisdom to handle the issues of life—small and large. The Holy Spirit is God on earth and God in us, so He will show Himself strong on behalf of the level of our faith, allowing Him to be Who He is in and for us.

I hope you caught me saying, *"Allow* Him to be," because even though He is God, He will not override our decision to choose or not choose His ways. He has created the earthly realm to be dealt with through mankind and given us the ability to choose right or wrong, life or death, Him or Satan. This is why, as born-again believers, we must have a kingdom mindset, as I have been saying in this chapter through the different examples that have been given.

Romans 12:2 shows us the need to be transformed by renewing our mind, and we know that God's Word is the only source for this renewal if we really want to develop "the kingdom mindset." Yet before we go after a renewed mind, as stated in this verse, we are told not to conform to this world. If our focus is on being like the world, then we are not going to focus on renewing the mind through the Word of God, which is most often going to be the opposite of how the world thinks.

As covered in chapter 4, one of the things that Satan is good at doing, as the god of this world system, is blinding the *minds* of those who don't believe lest they see the light of the gospel of Jesus Christ (2 Corinthians 4:4). He is the one who comes as a thief and a liar to deceive people and keep them in unbelief. However, that happens, and it ends up being a person's choice to make. This gives Satan permission to blind the mind because of the sin of unbelief. He is a master of deception, often twisting the truth and making it look and sound like the truth.

Jesus is the light of the world, and Satan, who is the darkness of this world, will do anything to make you miss, ignore, or reject the name of Jesus as the Christ, the Savior, the Lord of lords and King of kings, the Son of God, Who was raised from the dead. In Romans 10:13, we see that "for whosoever calls on the name of the Lord shall be saved." The light will come if you choose to call on Him, and blindness will have to go because it is really only a dark covering that Satan has been allowed to place through a person's choice (John 1:4–5). Now we can see a little more how critical it is, as a believer, to renew our minds with God's Word, giving it the first place and making it the final authority in our life's decisions.

I used to watch *Star Trek: The Next Generation*, and Captain Jean-Luc Picard would often speak of having to follow the "Prime Directive." Everything that they did had to follow the instructions of the "Prime Directive" as they explored the universe in their travels. He did not become the captain of that ship and crew, ignoring and rejecting the Prime Directive. That being said, our "Prime Directive" is the Word of God, and our captain is Jesus Christ, Who is giving us instructions on how to handle the travels of our lives in the kingdom and this world. We are the true aliens in this world because we are in this world but not of this world. We are citizens of the kingdom of heaven (Philippians 3:20–21).

In 2 Corinthians 5:20, Paul reveals that "we are Ambassadors of Christ," which means that we are His representatives in the kingdom on earth. We are His diplomatic agents on earth, and we represent the King of kings. We have been given the authority to speak on His behalf the word of the living God on earth. The power and authority of the Lord Jesus have been delegated to us, His ambassadors, to operate on earth and bring change to the world around us for the kingdom of God.

The ambassador has to have the kingdom mindset to be effective in that position and represent the King in every situation. You may look at yourself and say, How can someone like me be an ambassador of Christ? Well, the first thing you and I have to stop doing is looking at ourselves but looking at Jesus instead. Every time I look at myself, I need to THINK, SEE, and SAY, "I am my Father's son." This is what God the Father THINKS, SEES, and SAYS about me. Yes, He is saying, "You are my beloved son [this means daughters as well] whom I dearly love." You have chosen to believe in His Son, so you and Jesus are in the Father, and the Holy Spirit is in you. He is empowering us to *be* who He says we are through His grace and great love for us. So we must *be* persuaded and confident in His greatness in us to make it so.

Step into that place that He has prepared for you—yes, you. It is a place that God has tailor-made just for you, and no one else can have that place (Ephesians 2:10). Each of us was fearfully and wonderfully made, and His thoughts of us (individually) are more in number than the sand (Psalm 139:14–18). Let the King's mindset about you be your mindset about yourself, and let the Word of God be the final authority on the matter. In other words, believe what He's saying and then say, "And nothing else matters." Amen. So be it.

What would it be like to live one day at a time, increasing in "the kingdom mindset"? There would be so much more life for us to receive in our daily lives if we see it as He sees it and believe it as He believes it. It's time to "come up higher" in all that we are in Him until "nothing else matters." The Holy Spirit is waiting to make it so. What's holding you back? Hebrews 10:38–39 reminds us that we just live by faith, and if we draw back and shrink in fear, He has no pleasure in us doing so. But that's not our way. We don't draw back in fear of being destroyed because we believe, and by faith, our lives are saved. This is the reason we must have "the kingdom mindset" because we will draw back in fear if we don't see it from His perspective.

Ephesians 2:6 lets us know that one of the things that God has done is to raise us up together with Christ and make us have joint seating with Him in the heavenly realm where He sits in authority and power at the right hand of the Father. I asked the Lord, "Why do you want us to be seated with Him there in heaven while we are still here on earth?"

He said, "Because I want you to see things from My perspective."

It always looks different when we can see the situation from a viewpoint from above, looking down on the situation versus seeing it from the same level and viewpoint as everyone else. Jesus always saw things from the Father's perspective, and He could always clearly take the next steps in His journey to the cross and beyond (John 5:19, 30). Praise be to our Lord and Savior, Jesus Christ. I want to be just like Him, and He wants me to be just like Him too

(John 14:12). We ask in Jesus's name that we may be seen and known in His likeness as He is seen and known in the likeness of our Father in heaven. This is the purpose of having the kingdom mindset.

Therefore, Father, we pray that we gain more and more revelation of what it means to have the mind of Christ so that we may hold the thoughts (feelings and purposes) of His heart (AMPC) as we grow in grace and the knowledge of our Lord and Savior Jesus Christ. To Him be the glory both now and forever (1 Corinthians 2:16, 2 Peter 3:18). Amen.

Chapter 6

Increase—"Our New Normal"

The one thing I have constantly seen in the birth and growth of the Coming Up Higher Ministry is that it is the desire of Father God's heart for mankind to *increase*. The definition of *increase* is to grow, to be enlarged, to make progress, to prosper, become more, greater, to advance. Some have called this the law of increase where, in God's kingdom, there is always a call to make progress to advance from one point to another in life in "coming up higher." We can see this in 2 Corinthians 3:17–18 (AMPC). It reveals God's plan for us to increase, and this is not just a one-time blessing; throughout our eternal life, we will continually be transfigured into the image of Christ from one degree of glory to another. This comes from the Lord, Who is the Spirit.

We see it again in Romans 1:17, where the righteousness of God is revealed from faith to faith. In these two scriptures, we are coming up higher in faith and in the image of His glory. Our everyday living compels us to move toward something better than before in some way, small or large. We are always looking for a way to add to our lives something more or better to even maintain what we already have while growing up or to keep moving things forward. In life, the process of addition can be elementary, but it is necessary because where there is a subtraction, there will be a need for addition to continue living.

In His word, Father God is always encouraging us to believe and see that we are to grow stronger and have greater faith. We are called to prosper and make progress, and there is more to receive because He tells us that He is the God of more than enough (Ephesians 3:20). In Luke 2:52, we see that at twelve years old, it is stated that Jesus *kept* increasing in wisdom, in stature, and in favor with God and men. Yes, you can go to any Bible concordance and find scripture after scripture that proves this to be true throughout the Bible. He reveals this revelation to us from the very essence of our everyday life. He is here to reveal to us His loving heart so that we may learn more and more (increase in knowing) and see His heart more and more.

For example, have you ever wondered why life begins a new journey after becoming a Christ*ian* and after being what Jesus called being "born again"? Nicodemus was like most of us in hearing Jesus say, "Most assuredly, I say to you, unless one is born again, he cannot see the kingdom of God." Then Nicodemus said to Him, "How can a man be born when he is old? Can he enter a second time into his mother's womb and be born?" (John 3:3–4). Even in this discussion, we see the progression of how life is given for it to increase in us naturally and spiritually.

In John 10:10 (TPT), Jesus said, "A thief has only one thing in mind—he wants to steal, slaughter, and destroy. But I have come to give you everything in abundance, more than you expect—life in its fullness until you overflow!" In this verse, He shows us that the thief (Satan) comes to cause us to decrease, but He (the Lord) came to bring *increase* to us till we overflow. In this culture, we are faced with the Antichrist spirit of deception coming to bring the spirit of *wokeness* into our society, causing it to decrease into lawlessness.

In the Word of God, we have the spirit of truth coming to awaken us to the life of increase, bringing the truth that sets us free to receive life and life more abundantly, according to His divine order, which brings with it "the blessing." The choice we face is between the thief who has come to decrease us from life and take us toward death and the Lord Who has come to increase us toward life and redeem us from the curse of death. He even gives us life more abundantly. So choose life!

From the moment of conception in the mother's womb, as human beings, we have a God-given right to *increase* (grow) in our natural life and even choose eternal life. This means to eternally increase our belongingness to and knowledge of God our Father, as was intended from the very beginning of time (John 17:3, Psalm 139:13–16). Throughout the scriptures, we see God establishing a divine order that spelled out *increase*. When God began to bring the divine order of heaven and earth, working for six days and resting on the seventh day, He started the process of *increase* that persists even in our present understanding and observation. The creation of light, the heavens, water, vegetation, life in the waters, and life on land, including mankind, has never ceased to continue to be and has increased throughout time as we know it (Genesis 1:3–31).

What was the first thing that God said to mankind after He created them, male and female? In Genesis 1:28 (NKJV), "God blessed them, and God said to them, Be fruitful, multiply, and fill the earth and subdue it and have dominion over the fish of the sea, over the birds of the air and over every living thing that moves on the earth." If that's not a command to increase, then nothing is!

When we look at Genesis 2, we see even more of how God established the perfect life through the law of increase when He planted the garden of Eden and placed man (Adam) there in it (vv. 7–8). Everything was designed to be an ongoing path for growth and produce out of the ground without effort, all that was needed for a perfect and progressive pattern of increase as the normal way of life. All of life's needs were supplied and made a part of His divine order to establish the ongoing process of *increase*.

If you need more evidence, I want to encourage you to read through the Bible from Genesis to Revelation and focus on looking for the theme *increase*. You can't miss it because it's everywhere. It is such a powerful law existing in the realm of human beings that Satan has manipulated it to try to increase the evil he has brought into the earthly realm. Remember that it is a law, so it can be used for good or evil, depending on a person's choice. The adversary works to increase mankind toward death and evil, lawlessness, and disorder (chaos) so he can steal, kill, and destroy the life and the blessing that God spoke over mankind from the very beginning, as we saw above in Genesis 1:28. Satan hates the divine order that God has created for us to eternally live in, and he will try to do everything possible to keep us from having what is already ours through Jesus Christ, our Lord, our Champion, our King.

So why is *increase* our "new normal"? To have a new normal requires having a new mental perspective of this life. This takes us back to what Jesus said in John 10:10b (TPT): "I have come to give you everything in abundance, more than you expect—life in its fullness until it overflows." He has given us His life with a promise of a constant increase in abundant life, which is He Himself, for He is the Way, the Truth, and the Life (John 14:6). Now we are called into this new life in Him so that our hearts and minds will be renewed to this truth as our "new normal." It is revealed in 2 Corinthians 5:17 (AMPC], "Therefore if any person is [ingrafted] in Christ [the Messiah] he is a new creation (a new creature altogether); the old [previous moral and spiritual condition] has passed away. Behold, the fresh and new has come!"

This has happened to create in us a new path for us to grow and increase because "the fresh and new has come." It's now time to decrease from the old mindset of the life that has passed away and increase with the mindset of the new normal life that we have now received by being in Christ our Lord. We were created to increase in life in Him, and we must take on that mindset as "our new normal" while we are living in this life so we can acquire what He sacrificed His life for to have what God originally planned for us to have.

Paul said in Philippians 4:19 (AMPC), "And my God will liberally supply (fill to the full) your every need according to His riches in glory in Christ Jesus." Those supplies are found in Christ Jesus, where His riches of glory are waiting to be released into our lives to fulfill our every need, but this must be seen as "our new normal"; otherwise, we may miss out on the benefits that He has promised for us to have. The increase comes to create the mindset of this being "our new normal" so that we may grow in grace and the knowledge of our Lord and Savior Jesus Christ (2 Peter 3:18).

Don't miss out on what He has supplied just because you don't realize what now your "new normal" is in Him. Eternal life begins the moment you and I are born again into the life of Christ, Who promised us in John 3:16 that we would *have* eternal life, not at some future date. We would have it when we believe in Him, so be reminded that there is more to our life now than what we were used to having because now we know that *increase* is "our new normal." There is no shortcut to getting this new mindset.

The one thing I have learned in going after this exciting new normal way of thinking, seeing, and being, one that has access to God's plan of increase, is that I'm not going to get it my way. No matter how much I seek to get it working in my life, He will use the opportunity to draw me into Himself versus all the benefits that it brings. That's why in Matthew 6:33, Jesus tells us to seek first the kingdom of God and His righteousness, and *then* all these things will be added to us. For example, I mentioned in an earlier chapter, where Jesus said in John 15:7 (AMPC), "If you live in Me [abide vitally united to Me] and My words remain in you and continue to live in your hearts, ask whatever you will, and it shall be done for you." He is revealing to us something about how God works with us in "coming up higher" into His divine order.

He is not just trying to give us a better way to live in this world; He is showing us what is in His heart toward us and what our hearts really desire from life; it is not what we think. All that we are learning in these chapters is centered around one main thing: knowing God the Father and knowing God the Son, Who is Jesus Christ; the word *knowing* is an intimate term.

Look a little closer at the parts of John 15:7: "If you live in Me [this is a condition] and My words remain in you [this is more of the condition], then ask whatever you will, and it shall be done for you." Notice that this is a promise. Yes, a promise with a condition that shows us what God is really after. He's after you, your heart being filled with His Word and His presence. His word tells us all about Him and His heart. If you look closely enough, you will see a loving Father spending time with His child, reading to them and teaching them important things about the value of life and how to appreciate all that is available to them through His great love for them.

As that child learns the value and importance of all that's available to them, then they will see it, saying, "Ask whatever you will, and it will be done for you." As important as the law of increase is, it is of no good use without first knowing Him. This is the greatest desire of our Father, Who art in heaven. Matthew 6:9–13 (NKJV) tells us,

> Our Father in heaven, Hallowed be Your
> name.
> Your kingdom come. Your will be done.
> On earth as it is in heaven.
> Give us this day our daily bread.
> And forgive us our debts, as we forgive
> our debtors.
> And do not lead us into temptation but
> deliver us from the evil one.
> For Yours is the kingdom and the power
> and the glory forever. Amen.

If you can get the big picture of what is being revealed in this teaching, you will never read your Father's Word (the Bible) the same way again. The Father's heart will come off of those pages and speak nothing but love to you. Under the law in Joshua 1:8, the Lord told Joshua in the old covenant,

> This Book of the Law shall not depart
> from your mouth, but you shall meditate
> in it day and night, that you may observe
> to do according to all that is written in it.
> For then you will make your way prosper-
> ous, and then you will have good success.

This is yet another promise of God with instructions and conditions that required Joshua's ongoing attention, but it is with great benefits. Even though Joshua was not born again, God was still going after his heart being filled with the heart of God through His Word. Jesus is the Word of God for us, so we need to press into knowing Him and the Father, for this is the very definition of what eternal life is (John 17:3).

Today, we have the Holy Spirit living in us. He is the Master Teacher we need to fulfill the will of God in our lives, and it begins and continues eternally with knowing Him. So when we begin to grasp the true meaning of the value and worth of the law of increase and why it must become "our new normal," we must remember that it's all about "coming up higher" into an intimate knowledge of Father God and His Son, Jesus Christ, for this is what eternal life is all about.

If you're not experiencing a biblical increase in your life, don't blame God or anyone else for that matter because He has given us the power to succeed in our hands, and the Holy Spirit will be our coach if we allow Him to be. Begin today by saying, "Yes, Lord." Say yes to what He is revealing to you right now and watch Him advance you into the mindset of increase being your new normal.

Many years ago, I heard a pastor say, "When the student is ready, the teacher will appear." Selah! (Pause in His presence and think about it.)

Amen.

Chapter 7

I Have Come to Do Your Will, O God!

Everything that has been said in this book has to be concluded on the premise that we are making the choice to get in position for the will of God to be done in our lives. It is most important to realize that, from the very beginning, God's divine order for mankind was and yet is built upon His creative plan to have our lives in Christ Jesus. He is the only One Who knows what that means and how it must work for us all to excel in our lives by "coming up higher" in Him.

Remember that evil was not part of His plan for us; that's why He commanded Adam *not* to eat of the tree of the knowledge of good and evil. Everything God created, He saw that it was *good*, which is expanded in the Amplified Classic Version as "suitable, pleasant and He approved it." In another verse, *good* means "fitting, pleasant and He approved it" (Genesis 1:4, 10). God's way is perfect, and He makes our way perfect as we align ourselves with His way (Psalm 18:30, 32). As Christ*ians*, if we don't start here, then we haven't started at all because everything that a Christ*ian* is all about has to do with what Jesus said about Himself over and over again.

He said in John 6:38–40 (NKJV),

> For I have come down from heaven, not to do My own will, but the will of Him who sent Me.
>
> This is the will of the Father who sent Me, that of all He has given Me I should lose nothing but should raise it up at the last day.
>
> And this is the will of Him who sent Me, that everyone who sees the Son and believes in Him may have everlasting life; and I will raise him up at the last day.

His purpose for coming to earth and becoming a man was to fulfill the Father's will, and He goes on to reveal to us in verses 39 to 40 what that will was and yet is today. It was so that all of us who believed in Him would have everlasting life and be raised on the last day. If it were not for Him being relentlessly determined to do the Father's will,

I would not be writing this book, and you would not be reading it. Wow! How real is that statement?

He would be the furthest thing from our minds if He were there at all. Satan would not have been defeated, and the world would not have been overcome as we are told in the Scripture (Colossians 2:14–15, John 16:33). We would still be slaves to Satan and under the curse of the law, doomed for everlasting damnation and forever lost with no hope of salvation (Ephesians 2:1–3, 12; Galatians 3:13).

I will even take it a step further based on something Jesus said about God's Word. In Matthew 24:35 (TPT), Jesus said, "The earth and the sky will wear out and fade away before one word I speak loses its power or fails to accomplish its purpose." So Jesus lets us know that there is no way that the Word of God can or will be changed from what is written. When Satan tempted Jesus in Matthew 4:1–11, we see that all Jesus did in replying to what Satan had to say in his temptations was, "It is written." The written Word of God is eternal and cannot be touched. We see this being stated with finality in Psalm 138:2 (AMPC):

> I will worship toward Your holy temple and praise Your name for Your loving-kindness and for Your truth and faithfulness; for You have exalted above all else

Your name and Your word and You have magnified Your word above all Your name.

Do you see how much God honors His own word? He literally submits Himself to His own word. He is God, and He did *not* have to choose to be limited to His word. He could have kept Himself in a place where He couldn't be touched.

Therefore, the title of this chapter, "I Have Come to Do Your Will, O God," is taken from Hebrews 10:5–7 (NKJV), where it repeats what Jesus said,

> Therefore, when He came into the world,
> He said:
> Sacrifice and offering You did not desire,
> But a body You have prepared for Me.
> In burnt offerings and sacrifices for sin
> You had no pleasure.
> Then I said, "Behold, I have come—
> In the volume of the book, it is written of
> Me—
> To do Your will, O God."

To understand about this chapter, it would be most helpful for you to read the entire tenth chapter of Hebrews, so please take time to do that and capture the whole picture of why Christ was so adamant about doing His Father's will. It will show the reason we have a New Testament (covenant) since Jesus fulfilled the righteousness of God on our behalf and provided us with access to our Father in heaven. Also, God's wrath against our sin was satisfied completely.

The Word of God will always bring correction to the things that come to interfere with His divine order because His Word and His divine order are one and the same. There is a law/promise that comes to mind in Galatians 6:7: "Do not be deceived; God will not be mocked; for whatever a man sows, he will also reap." It lets us know that God's name, His plans, and His will—with all of this being tied to His word—will not be mocked, added to, or taken away from by anyone. Instead, whatever anyone tries to do will be done to them instead. This is a law of God, activated based on what is sown. Therefore, be aware of what you are sowing, especially if it is in conflict with God's Word.

At times, it may seem to us that those things are out of control or that the things happening are advancing in the wrong direction. However, we must remember that He is God and has all authority and all power in His hand. How He chooses to handle what does or doesn't happen from our point of view does not change that *truth*. Take notice that I didn't use the term *fact*, but I said *truth*. We live in a world full of facts about everything to the point that we often use the phrase "the facts of life" as a way to discuss life.

There are many true things in the way of facts, but if the facts I have disagree with the truth, then I must defer to the truth, not the facts. Facts are tied to what is known about a subject matter, and truth is the reality of that subject beyond the known facts. Therefore, the truth must supersede the knowledge of the facts, and the facts will eventually catch up with and be absorbed by the truth (1 Corinthians 13:8–10 AMPC). A good example of this is found in ancient days when there was an argument about whether the earth was flat or spherical (round). The ancient Greeks were in debate for centuries about this question, and finally, updated facts continued to bring the argument to the place where it was agreed with scriptures like Isaiah 40:21–22 (AMPC):

> [You worshipers of idols, you are without excuse.] Do you not know? Have you not heard? Has it not been told you from the beginning? [These things ought to convince you of God's omnipotence and of the folly of bowing to idols.] Have

you not understood from the foundations of the earth? [Romans 1:20–21]

It is God Who sits above the circle [the horizon] of the earth, and its inhabitants are like grasshoppers; it is He Who stretches out the heavens like [gauze] curtains and spreads them out like a tent to dwell in.

Even without looking at this scripture on that matter, look up and see that the sun, moon, and other planets are all round. Why would God make the earth flat, and who has traveled around the world and come to the end of the distance where you can go no farther? When the ship sails off into the horizon, does it stop because it came to the end of that direction, or can it sail on until it comes back around to the starting point? You may be asking why I have chosen this as a subject matter. One reason is that there is a new movement in today's culture called the Flat Earth Society, saying that they believe now that the earth is flat again, and the movement is growing. They are trying to make people go back to believing that the earth is flat after almost two thousand years of science that proves otherwise. Facts can go back and forth with what is or what isn't because they are always evolving with added knowledge to the last facts at hand until, somewhere along the way, they catch up with the truth, which is eternal.

We will see more of this kind of confusion growing in our culture because all it takes is for something to go viral on social media, and this generation will take it and run with it before the *facts* are investigated. We can't wait for the truth to be known before everyone gives their expert opinion about it. Then by the time the truth finally comes out, the damage has already been done, distorting what really took place.

In 1 John 4:4–6 (AMPC), we are given a revelation of what will happen if humanity follows the path of false prophets. These are the agents of the Antichrist spirit (v. 4), and we must discern what spirit it is before we open up to and receive its voice. Is it the spirit of truth or the spirit of error, as stated in verse 6 below?

> Little children, you are of God [you belong to Him] and have [already] defeated and overcome them [the agents of the antichrist], because He Who lives in you is greater [mightier] than he who is in the world.
>
> They proceed from the world and are of the world; therefore, it is out of the world [its whole economy morally consid-

ered] that they speak, and the world listens (pays attention) to them.

We are [children] of God. Whoever is learning to know God [progressively to perceive, recognize, and understand God by observation and experience, and to get an ever-clearer knowledge of Him] listens to us; and he who is not of God does not listen or pay attention to us. By this we know (recognize) the Spirit of Truth and the spirit of error.

I have been sharing these things with you because the Holy Spirit drew me into these examples before I realized all that was being said on this subject matter. I felt compelled to at least touch the fact that leads us right back to the truth of why Jesus was compelled to do His Father's will no matter what. Jesus said in John 5:19 and 30 (AMPC) that He can do nothing of Himself but only does what He sees the Father doing. John 5:30 takes us deeper into the depth of His obedience.

I am able to do nothing from Myself [independently, of My own accord—but only as I am taught by God and as I get His orders]. Even as I hear, I judge [I decide as I am bidden to decide. As the voice comes to Me, so I give a decision], and My judgment is right [just, righteous], because I do not seek or consult My own will [I have no desire to do what is pleasing to Myself, My own aim, My own purpose] but only the will and pleasure of the Father Who sent Me.

I was not going to put into my own words what He is saying here because it's too rich in meaning not to put your eyes on it.

Note: It is very important for us, as believers, to put our own eyes on the written word versus using memory or paraphrasing scripture. There are times when we must do that for the sake of time, but I encourage you to practice putting your eyes on the Word of God, and you will see the difference it makes in your ability to see more and more revelation of the truth. We cannot afford to rely only on what we have learned over the years, for the Holy Spirit is revealing to us more and more as we stay teachable and dependent on His Word, showing us what is to come. The will of God is the Word of God, and yet we need the Holy

Spirit to help us know what He is doing on earth in each season of time until He comes for us.

Jesus had to maintain the highest level of truth in what He said and did. He could not allow Himself to be out of place with the prophetic word spoken about what the Messiah would do when He came. He had to fulfill every prophecy's exact meaning and order to qualify as the true Messiah. It is said that there were at least three hundred fulfilled prophecies about Him coming as the Lamb of God. He is coming again to fulfill the rest of what must happen in His second coming.

In Hebrews 10:9–10, Jesus tells us that one of the main things He did was take away the first covenant and establish the second one so He could take away the sins of the world once and for all. He gave all of us the option to become a child of God if we'd choose to believe in Him. See verses 9–10 (AMPC):

> He then went on to say, Behold, [here]
> I am, coming to do Your will. Thus He
> does away with and annuls the first (for-
> mer) order [as a means of expiating sin]
> so that He might inaugurate and establish
> the second (latter) order [Psalm 40:6–8]

And in accordance with this will [of God], we have been made holy [consecrated and sanctified] through the offering made once for all of the body of Jesus Christ [the Anointed One].

God's will being done also benefited Him, as shown in Colossians 1:20:

> And God purposed that through [by the service, the intervention of] Him [the Son] all things should be completely reconciled back to Himself, whether on earth or in heaven, as through Him, [the Father] made peace by means of the blood of His cross.

God made peace with us by accepting the payment of Jesus's blood on the cross. This is the only sacrifice that could wash away our sins and satisfy the wrath of God toward the sins of mankind. Now He can freely give to us the gift of salvation, eternal life, by grace through our faith.

The position we take in all of this is to keep increasing our faith by exercising the Word of God in love and with a heart kept before Him. We can grow where we are, like

King David, who was said to be a man after God's own heart. I see this as initially having a heart that goes after the heart of God to the point that He fills our hearts, making it look like the heart of God, or we are recognized as a son who has his Father's heart.

In 1 Samuel 13:13–14, we are told that the Lord sought out a man after His own heart. I believe He is yet seeking to find those who are after His own heart. David honors God's Word; he was a wholehearted worshiper. He walked in obedience (most of his life), and he trusted God to receive mercy and justice whenever it was needed and required. The thing God was looking for even then was someone who would commit to following His will; that's why King Saul was removed from that position because he disobeyed God's command, as seen in verse 13. David loved God with all his heart and soul and gave himself to God in every way, leading the people of God during his reign as king.

David is an example of one who gives himself doing the will of God as king over the tribes of Israel, and God honored his diligence in doing so. Let us take note that this is still what God looks for in the heart of men today—our wholehearted dedication in every area of our lives.

In conclusion, coming up higher gives life to all the things we have been sharing with you in this book. It is a driving force of being a disciple of Christ, with our aim focused on being like Him in every area of our lives. This life's journey will only be accomplished if we stay in position with our whole hearts lifted to Him each day for the rest of our lives. Maybe that's why the first and greatest commandment is to love the Lord your God with all of your heart, all your soul, all of your mind, and all of your strength (Mark 12:30).

We are all faced with decisions and choices that will either increase or decrease us toward that mark of the high calling in Christ Jesus. Apostle Paul said in Philippians 3:10 (AMPC), "[For my determined purpose is] that I may know Him [that I may progressively become more deeply and intimately acquainted with Him, perceiving and recognizing and understanding the wonders of His person more strongly and more clearly]." In verse 12 of the same chapter, he states that he has not already attained [this ideal] or has already been made perfect, but he presses on to lay hold of it and make it his own because Christ held him and made him His own.

He continues to say in verses 13–14 that we must forget those things behind us, reach forward with all diligence to what lies ahead, and press on toward the goal to win the prize of our high calling of God in Christ Jesus. The high call is to come up higher in Him one day at a time and maintain what we have learned for the glory of God.

I would like to finish this chapter with a scripture that sets the mindset we all must adhere to as born-again believers if we want to walk in the victory we have been given by our Lord and Savior, Jesus Christ. Paul reveals this mindset in the verses below.

> But thanks be to God, Who gives us the victory [making us conquerors] through our Lord Jesus Christ.
>
> Therefore, my beloved brethren, be firm [steadfast], immovable, always abounding in the work of the Lord [always being superior, excelling, doing more than enough in the service of the Lord], knowing and being continually aware that your labor in the Lord is not futile [it is never wasted or to no purpose]. (1 Corinthians 15:57–58 AMPC)

May His Word forever be the final authority in all the matters in our life.

Amen. So be it!

Born and raised in a Christian home, J. Alfred Wright became a born-again Christian at the age of nine. He is a husband and father and is married to Rebecca K. Wright, with children and grandchildren. He had a love and talent for music and became a musician and singer in church. He worked with choirs and praise-and-worship groups in the ministry of music. At age 18, he realized that his love for God's Word had drawn him into teaching and ministering the Word to others. At age 28, he was ordained as a minister; and at age 32, an ordained Elder. He completed Bible study courses at Moody Bible Institute and Liberty University, and he continued to grow in a love for God's Word. He has over forty-five years of ministry as a musician and teacher of the Word and over twenty years in the prison ministry.

In 2018, he and his wife began Coming Up Higher Ministry Outreach. Their goal is to show forth the heart of God, calling us to take our Christianity to a new level in being and doing the Word of God. He knows this will only be accomplished by the work of the Holy Spirit working in us one day at a time as we journey through life.